THE
ISLES OF SHOALS
REMEMBERED

THE
ISLES OF SHOALS
REMEMBERED

A LEGACY FROM AMERICA'S
FIRST MUSICIANS' AND ARTISTS' COLONY

Introduced with Text by Caleb Mason

Charles E. Tuttle Company, Inc.

Boston • Rutland, Vermont • Tokyo

PHOTO CREDITS

Courtesy of the University of New Hampshire, Isles of Shoals Collection:
  Photo of Ross Turner, William Mason, John Appleton Brown, John Knowles Paine, and William Winch (January 14 entry)'
  Photo of William Mason (January 22 entry)
  Photo of Celia Thaxter with son John (February 6 entry)
  Photo of Childe Hassam (March month-head)
  Photo of Oscar Laighton's Schooner Drawing (April 7 entry)
  Photo of Celia Thaxter's Parlor (November 18 entry)
  Photo of John Knowles Paine (November 22 entry)
  Photo of view from Celia Thaxter's piazza (December 25 entry)

Courtesy of the New York Public Library:
  Photo of Ignace Jan Paderewski (June 1 entry)
  Photo of Teresa Carreño (December 18 entry)

Courtesy of the Perkins School for the Blind, Watertown, Massachusetts:
  Photo of Helen Keller (July 14)

From Private Collection:
  Autograph of Robert Schumann (January 22 entry)
  Autograph of Richard Wagner (January 22 entry)
  Photo of Ossip Gabrilowitsch (February 1 entry)
  Photo of Mason and Thomas Quartet (February 11 entry)
  Photo of Daniel Gregory Mason (February 26 entry)
  Photo of Theodore Thomas (September 4 entry)
  Photo of Arthur Whiting (December 7 entry)

Cover illustration by Ignaz Marcel Gaugengigl

Published by the Charles E. Tuttle Company, Inc. of Rutland, Vermont
& Tokyo, Japan with editorial offices at 77 Central Street, Boston, Massachusetts 02109

Library of Congress Cataloging-in-Publication Data

Isles of Shoals Remembered: A Legacy from America's First Musicians' and Artists'
Colony/introduced with text by Caleb Mason.
        p.   cm.
    Includes bibliographical references (p.   ).
    ISBN 0-8048-1776-6 (hardcover: acid-free paper).
    1. Artist colonies – Isles of Shoals (Me. and N.H.) 2. Arts, American – Isles of
    Shoals (Me. and N.H.) 3. Arts, Modern – 19th century – Isles of Shoals (Me.
    and N.H.) 4. Artists – Isles of Shoals (Me. and N.H.) – Biography. I. Mason,
    Caleb, 1955-   .
NX505.I84 1992   91-67338
700'.9741'95 – dc20   CIP

First printing 1992
PRINTED IN THE UNITED STATES

IN RESEARCHING WILLIAM MASON'S ORIGINAL 1901 DAYBOOK, which forms the basis of this book, I have been pleasantly surprised at the wealth of information available on the contributors. I have elected not to burden what is intended to be an informative text with footnotes, as I feel this would interfere with the appearance of the book. Therefore, I have cited significant source materials in the Bibliography and hope readers will want to explore the many entertaining works available. Any student of the Isles of Shoals owes a tremendous amount of thanks to Lyman Rutledge for his book *The Isles of Shoals in Lore and Legend* and to Celia Thaxter's granddaughter, Rosamond Thaxter, for her informative work *Sandpiper: The Life and Letters of Celia Thaxter*.

Other significant books that I have referred to are: *Our American Music* by John Tasker Howard; *The Great Pianists from Mozart to the Present* and *The Great Conductors* by Harold C. Schonberg; and William Mason's *Memories of a Musical Life*. Joseph Lash's outstanding biography *Helen and Teacher* was invaluable in researching the Helen Keller entry, and offered one of the more entertaining diversions experienced while researching the contributors.

Of the total of 365 original daybook entries in William Mason's 1901 daybook, I have selected 53 of the most notable for inclusion in this book. I would like to thank my publisher, Peter Ackroyd, for his vision in determining how the original material could best be put together in a new daybook form. It was his suggestion to show the original daybook pages exactly as they appeared, but on a larger format page that would allow for supplementary photos and text. His courage and commitment are greatly appreciated. My agent, Helen Pratt, never gave up in her belief in the possibilities for this project. Eleanor Perényi kindly offered a professional writer's critique of the first draft of my introduction that helped me enormously, and my mother, Millie, and wife, Anne, each offered valuable comments on the text material. I received a great deal of encouragement from the dedicated people at the Boston Museum of Fine Arts, the Archives of American Art, and several other institutions and libraries who generously shared their knowledge with me.

The design and production of this book presented many challenges, and I'd like to extend special thanks to Linda Smith, the book's editor, and to Mary Reed, the book's designer. Mary brought to this project an unusual combination of design sense and technical knowledge of the latest desktop computer tools. With the assistance of her colleagues at ImageSet Design in Portland, Maine, she was able to electronically enhance much of the original material and control the many prepress variables that often frustrate publisher and author.

Every effort has been made to have the original daybook entries fall in date sequence with the corresponding facing pages. In the majority of cases this has been possible. However, the overall layout has been dictated by the original daybook's sequence, so I hope readers can bear with those instances where the original entry does not correspond to the facing page's dates.

I clearly recall the first time I looked through the original daybook. What an incredible work it was, and even more incredible that it had survived so well for nearly an entire century. As I researched the contributors' lives, a feel for the time period began to emerge from this innocently produced slice of social history. I began to think that by using the original material as a point of departure, I could present throughout the course of one year a feel for a great time period in the American arts. And in the process, I could ensure that parts of the precious original daybook would be preserved for many people to enjoy, instead of confining it to a box in the attic.

Now I am delighted to realize the goal of seeing many of the original daybook pages reproduced, and hope that the joy I initially found in being greeted by the surprise on every page will be a pleasure shared by others. I also hope that modern readers will come to appreciate better an important period in the history of American arts.

This book belongs to the original contributors whose spirit of friendship shines through on every page and whose gift is not forgotten but lives on within the pages that follow.

All nature's musical voices
Whispered, "Awake and see!
Awake, for the day rejoices!"
What news had the morn for me?

From *At Dawn* by
Celia Thaxter

CHRISTMAS DAY IN THE YEAR 1900 must have been a very special day for the American musician, William Mason. On this day he received a remarkable gift, an original daybook for the year 1901 that his musical and artistic friends associated with poet Celia Thaxter's arts colony on the Isles of Shoals had created for him. As he turned each page he was greeted by a surprise, ranging from a watercolor by Childe Hassam to several bars of music from Edward MacDowell. Every day of the year featured something special for him to see.

The 1901 daybook was a rare labor of love, an ambitious and time-consuming undertaking the likes of which would be unthinkable in our hurried modern world. Coordinated by Celia Thaxter's sister-in-law, Julia Laighton, 365 individual daybook pages with only the day of the week and month hand-drawn across the top of each page were sent to the various artists and musicians Mason knew. Back they came, each inscribed in a unique manner, to be bound together in a handsome red leather cover. Many of the contributors Mason had come to know during his annual summer vacations at the Appledore Hotel on Appledore Island, one of the Isles of Shoals, located ten miles off the Maine/New Hampshire coast. During the idle summers of the 1880s many of America's most distinguished people could be found relaxing in Celia Thaxter's cottage, just a short walk from the hotel. Thaxter held in a charming and informal way a remarkable salon in which art, music, and literature were celebrated in an invigorating natural setting. This salon was the first of its kind in America, a precursor to the many artists' colonies that flourished during the early twentieth century.

Among the more notable entries to the 1901 daybook was a watercolor by Childe Hassam for the month of October. Hassam, one of America's foremost impressionist painters, maintained a studio on Appledore where several of his finest works were painted. Ignaz Gaugengigl, the Bavarian-born artist who was one of Hassam's earliest teachers in Boston and a regular visitor to Appledore, contributed two detailed drawings of a flutist and violinist, enhancing the overall musical nature of the daybook. And Ross Turner, who like Hassam had a studio near Thaxter's cottage, provided two watercolors, including a lovely scene of Mexico for the month of September.

The musical entries included several bars of music from Edward MacDowell, who came to Appledore often with his wife. Other musicians with whom Mason crossed paths during his career who were not associated with Appledore also submitted pages to the daybook. Among these is a personal greeting from Ignace Jan Paderewski, the Polish romantic pianist who was the great headliner of his time. Two other popular pianists, Ossip Gabrilowitsch and Teresa Carreño, each sent in musical greetings. And several of America's first generation of serious classical musicians provided entries, including Theodore Thomas, Dudley Buck, and Horatio Parker.

Helen Keller contributed a brief passage using her raised writing board. As a freshman entering Radcliffe in 1900, the deaf and blind Keller was capturing the hearts of many prominent Bostonians who were impressed by her special gifts. How Keller came to contribute to the daybook is somewhat of a mystery, although it is possible that one of her benefactors, Laurence Hutton, may have offered the opportunity. Hutton and his wife visited Appledore on several occasions, and each sent William Mason their greetings in the daybook. Laurence Hutton was a writer and historian whose book *Talks in a Library with Laurence Hutton* recounted his important discussions with leading Americans, ranging from President Grover Cleveland to author Mark Twain.

Celia Thaxter's family sent its greetings from Appledore. Celia had died in 1894, but her brothers Cedric and Oscar Laighton continued to operate the Appledore Hotel. The Laighton family's involvement with the Isles of Shoals began in 1839 when Celia's father, Thomas Laighton, turned his back on a promising political career (he had been elected to the New Hampshire Senate in 1837) to accept the seemingly insignificant job as keeper of the White Island lighthouse. Leaving mainland culture behind, Laighton moved his family to White Island, a desolate "rock" where the power of many fierce winter storms would leave a lasting impression on young Celia Laighton. Only four years old when her family moved to White Island, Celia was raised in a transcendentalist household where her father assumed responsibility for her education. Growing up in almost complete isolation, with the island birds and flowers as her constant companions, Celia firmly established the roots of her own sensitivity to all living things, which was to become her personal hallmark.

In 1847, Celia's father moved the family from White Island to Appledore Island, the largest of the Isles of Shoals. Apparently keeping the light at White Island had grown tedious, and Laighton now set his sights on a larger ambition, building a resort hotel on Appledore. Enlisting the help of his good friend Levi Thaxter, the two men pooled their diverse talents in opening the Appledore Hotel in 1848, the first of the fashionable summer hotels that would spring up in later years all along the Atlantic seaboard. The partnership was to be short-lived, dissolved after the first season when the outraged Thomas Laighton discovered Levi's sudden romantic interest in his fourteen-year-old Celia.

Thaxter, who had been assisting Laighton with Celia's tutoring, recognized early on that his pupil possessed an unusual intellect. Celia was most likely in awe of her older teacher's worldliness. The

Harvard-educated Thaxter introduced Celia to the works of Edgar Allan Poe, Robert Browning, and other writers whose books were not available in her father's library. Isolated for so many years from mainland culture, this other world that Thaxter suddenly offered must have been very enticing to Celia. Celia had blossomed into a striking beauty, and what had begun innocently as mutual affection between teacher and pupil quickly became something much larger. Despite her father's objections, Celia and Levi were married in September of 1851 when Celia was only sixteen.

Many distinguished writers, including Henry David Thoreau, John Greenleaf Whittier, James Russell Lowell, and Nathaniel Hawthorne, came to stay at the Appledore Hotel shortly after it opened. Hawthorne offered in his *American Notebook* a glimpse of Celia as she appeared shortly after her marriage. "We found Mrs. Thaxter sitting in a neat little parlor, very simply furnished, but in good taste. She is not now more than eighteen years old, very pretty, and with the manners of a lady—not prim and precise—but with enough of freedom and ease."

Celia's unaffected manner, her "freedom and ease," was a characteristic that attracted many people to her. Her poetry spoke of the simple sights and sounds she knew so well as she observed her island surroundings. Somehow Celia managed to find time to write poetry despite the burdens of her domestic chores, which included raising three children, one of whom was mildly retarded. Her first poem, *Land-Locked*, was published by the *Atlantic* in 1861 when she was twenty-six. Levi Thaxter gave the poem to the *Atlantic*'s first editor, James Russell Lowell, who had been a classmate of his at Harvard. Lowell gave the poem its title and published it immediately. Lowell's successor at the *Atlantic*, James Fields, published many of Celia's poems during his years as editor. Fields displayed a rare publishing genius in introducing American readers to the works of fireside poets Whittier, Longfellow, Holmes, and Lowell. Celia was good friends throughout her life with Fields and his wife, Annie.

By the beginning of the 1880s, Celia had become one of America's most popular poets. Her poems *Sandpiper* and *The Sunrise Never Failed Us Yet*, along with her first work of prose, *Among the Isles of Shoals*, had gained her a wide readership. As an indication of how popular she was, her publisher rejected Emily Dickinson's first submission because they already had a "female poet" on their list. During the 1880s hundreds of visitors would flock to the Appledore Hotel, hoping to catch a glimpse of the "Island Queen" as she presided over the many admirers in her parlor; however, only a select group of the paying guests at the hotel were included in Celia's circle.

Typically, on a hot midsummer's afternoon, her friends would stroll over from the nearby hotel, passing through Celia's magnificent garden before entering the parlor quietly so as not to disturb her as she sat writing at her desk. Celia's dark green parlor was furnished with long sofas and easy chairs, comfortable furniture on which her friends could sit as she recited one of her poems, or as one of the gifted musical guests played Beethoven or Chopin sonatas on her grand piano. Every inch of wall space was covered with paintings by Childe Hassam, Ross Turner, John Appleton Brown, and other artists and friends. Artists hopeful of making a sale displayed their works on the many easels set up in the room. Beautifully coordinated flower arrangements from Celia's cottage garden added color and fragrance to the sun-splashed room. (A guest claimed to have counted 110 different flowers in the parlor one day.) Looking out across the ocean, the mainland would disappear from view in the midday haze, heightening the guests' sense of being lost within the security of island living.

Thaxter's garden was a brilliant array of old-fashioned flowers that she nurtured with keen sensitivity gained through a lifetime of exploration and discovery. The recent reissue of her gardening classic, *An Island Garden*, with the original illustrations by Childe Hassam, has found a welcoming audience. Much of the reissue's success can be attributed to Thaxter's poetic approach to gardening. Thaxter's garden was in a sense one of her greatest poetic triumphs, giving constant joy to all who were privileged to see it, a joy that was simple on the surface yet belied the enormous amount of work and know-how that went into orchestrating its beauty. Thaxter's frequent talks with her plants, a cause of much amusement for onlookers, may have magically coaxed them to bloom in ways others could only hope for. As was true of the musicians who claimed they never performed better than when in her company, the same could be said for her green friends in the garden.

Childe Hassam took full advantage of the appealing landscapes to be found at Appledore. Celia Thaxter had been an art student of his in Boston during the early 1880s, and they were to form a deep friendship that lasted until her death. Celia's garden, overflowing with informal masses of delphiniums, phlox, hollyhocks, and poppies, offered Hassam a setting not unlike that of Monet's Giverny. Two of Hassam's most famous paintings, *The Room with Flowers* and *Coast Scene, Isles of Shoals*, were painted while at Appledore. The former was painted in 1894, the year Thaxter died, and shows Hassam at his impressionist best as the vases filled with flowers inside Celia's parlor blend together with the barely discernible figure of a woman (possibly Hassam's wife, Maud) reclining on the sofa.

Music often could be heard coming from Celia's parlor. Several of her poems describe the sublime effect of music on the listener. During the 1860s, Lowell Mason, the American hymn composer and musical educator, introduced his children to Appledore where his son William became a regular at the piano. On several occasions, John Knowles Paine, America's first symphonic composer, and William Mason would play the piano as recounted in the following excerpt from Celia Thaxter's letter to her friend Rose Lamb:

Last night was like a dream. All the days now are exquisite, the sun rises and sets like a crimson cannon-ball, and the colors are indescribably beautiful. And the moon at night, and the soft airs and hazy stars, all things make me wish for you more and more. . . . Paine and Mason played Beethoven duets last evening; it was fine. Then Mason played alone, and then Paine. . . . As I came over, the light was exquisite, the half moon red and warm in mid-heaven, and the west faintly luminous; the tide very high and full, the waves whispering, the south wind blowing softly; the tall hollyhocks stirring gently against the sea and sky, the masses of leaves and flowers in the garden dusky and dim—all so quiet.

In William Mason's *Memories of a Musical Life*, published in 1901, he described his vantage point from the piano bench:

It was a pleasure being so much at Appledore to play a great deal in these informal ways. The doors wide open to the sun and salt breezes, the people sitting in the room and grouped on the piazza, shaded by its lovely vines, the beautiful vistas of gaily colored flowers, sea and sky beyond, made a charming and ever-to-be-remembered scene.

As a young boy, William Mason had accompanied his father, Lowell, on many of his pioneering musical conventions aimed at raising American musical standards. Lowell performed a critical service in this regard, with one of his finest achievements coming in 1836 when he convinced the Boston school board to include music as a subject in the public school curriculum, footing the bill himself for the first year. The determination of Lowell Mason to educate Americans about serious music during the first half of the nineteenth century would be ably carried forward by his son, William, during the second half.

During the mid-nineteenth century, what little classical music there was in America had arrived with the many foreign musicians who fled revolutions in Europe. In 1852, a popular musical event in New York was the appearance of Master Marsh, the four-year-old drummer who could play two drums at once. The first American orchestra, the New York Philharmonic Society, had opened in 1842 and consisted of part-time amateur musicians who oftentimes had to substitute whatever instruments they had for the composer's intended instrumentation.

It was against this backdrop that twenty-year-old William Mason set sail for Europe in 1849, where he met many of the great composers of the time including Franz Liszt, Robert Schumann, and Richard Wagner. Mason was Liszt's first American student and his eyewitness accounts of the early Liszt years at Weimar are important for the insights they provide of this rich musical period. (In fact, Mason's memoirs are the only ones to describe this period from the student's perspective.)

When Mason returned from Europe in 1854, he immediately set out on what were the first unaccompanied piano recitals in America. Mason performed for the first time in America works by Schumann, Brahms, and Liszt, often playing to near-empty halls in rural towns stretching between New York and Chicago. In addition to his efforts on the concert circuit, Mason took on many pupils, several of whom became the first American composers and performers to achieve international recognition.

It was at Appledore, in Celia Thaxter's parlor, that Mason introduced his captive audience to Edward MacDowell's *Tragica* sonata. He played the sonata once a day throughout an entire summer until it became a favorite of the guests. MacDowell dedicated his *Eroica* sonata to Mason in appreciation for his support. Mason's generosity in helping to further the careers of his pupils—as well as the many visiting foreign musicians he knew—was a kindness few forgot. It was in this same spirit of giving that his friends participated in the unique daybook he received on Christmas Day, 1900.

Mason kept the daybook with him at his Steinway Hall studio until his death in 1908. Probably no other personal belonging provided as much satisfaction, since it brought together at a glance the many people he had known during his lifetime. Now, nearly a hundred years after the original gift was presented to William Mason, several of the more notable entries are reproduced here for all to enjoy.

The title page of the original daybook, translated from the German as "The Year Dawning."

THOMAS ALLEN, JR. (1849-1924)

THOMAS ALLEN OFTEN PAINTED BARBIZON-INSPIRED, pastoral landscapes. He first exhibited at the National Academy of Design in 1876. Other exhibitions followed at the Paris Salon in 1882, 1887, and 1889, and in Boston at the Vose Galleries, Water Color Club, and Copley Society. Allen was a trustee and president of the Boston Museum of Fine Arts.

January

1

2

3

4

5

6

7

January

8

9

10

11

12

13

14

Back Row (l to r): Ross Turner, William Mason. Front Row (l to r): John Appleton Brown, John Knowles Paine, William Winch

MONDAY. JAN **14**

"Happy the man and happy he alone,
He who can call to day his own;
He who, secure within, can say,
Tomorrow, do thy worst; for I have
lived to day."   *Dryden.*

J. Appleton Brown.

JOHN APPLETON BROWN (1844-1902)

THE PAINTER JOHN APPLETON BROWN, here quoting from Dryden. Unfortunately the two Brown entries to the daybook have not survived in good enough condition to reproduce here. Brown's seascapes of New England were among the more popular paintings on display in Celia Thaxter's parlor. Born in Newburyport, Massachusetts, Brown studied in France at the age of twenty-one, where the works of Corot and Daubigny left a lasting impression on his style. His paintings are included in the Boston Museum of Fine Arts collection.

January

15

16

17

18

19

20

21

SUNDAY – JAN –

20

"Music, I imagine, ought to end in the love of the beautiful." Plato's "Republic"

Here written by R.W. Gilder

RICHARD WATSON GILDER (1844-1909)

THE AMERICAN POET AND EDITOR who visited Appledore, here quoting from Plato's *Republic*. In 1869-70, Gilder edited the magazine *Hours at Home*. This publication was absorbed by *Scribner's Monthly* in 1870, where Gilder eventually became editor in chief. In addition to his editing, Gilder wrote sixteen volumes of poetry.

January

22 ——————————————————————

23 ——————————————————————

24 ——————————————————————

25 ——————————————————————

26 ——————————————————————

William Mason

THURSDAY - JAN - 24

Wishes unnumbered wish I thee;
I send our greetings over the sea,-
Love without measure from the whole
Laighton family, Isles of Shoal (s).
If you could have as happy a time
As you've given to others in music's rhyme,
Most happy birthday would now be Thine.

Many, nations and many men
Answer in music To your pen,
Sounding a friend That's always True.-
On this bright day when you're seventy-two
Near' all the world cries 'We love you!"

WILLIAM MASON (1829-1908)

A PERSONAL GREETING FROM JULIA LAIGHTON'S FAMILY on Appledore. Julia Laighton did most of the legwork in compiling William Mason's daybook. She was married to Cedric Laighton, Celia Thaxter's brother.

One can only wonder what thoughts passed through William Mason's mind as he read this entry for his seventy-second birthday. With only seven years of life remaining, Mason was a widely acclaimed and feted musician who could look back over a long career that had witnessed tremendous change and growth in the American musical climate. Possibly his thoughts were transported back to the year 1849 when, as a young man of twenty, he had set out on the adventure of a lifetime, a trip to Europe to further his musical education.

He had intended to go directly to Leipzig to study with Moscheles. Arriving at Bremen, however, he learned that within the past few days there had been bloodshed in the streets of Leipzig. Julius Schuberth, an influential music publisher in Hamburg, was a fellow passenger and suggested he stay awhile with him in Hamburg. Following a quick trip to Paris, Mason visited Schuberth for a brief time, but long enough to give the publisher one of his compositions, *Les Perles de Rosée*, which in turn Schuberth presented to the great Hungarian pianist and composer, Franz Liszt.

Schuberth subsequently told Mason that Liszt had liked the piece. Seeing an opportunity, Mason wrote Liszt with hopes of becoming one of his students. Unfortunately, he misinterpreted his reply as a polite rebuff, and so unnecessarily waited four more years before finally visiting him in 1853.

In 1849 Mason knew nothing of Robert Schumann's music. Mendelssohn then dominated the musical world. At the second concert at the Gewandhaus in Leipzig that Mason attended, however, he was bowled over by a performance of Schumann's First Symphony. In his memoirs Mason writes:

> I was so wrought up by it that I hummed passages from it as I walked home, and sat down at the piano when I got there, and played as much of it as I could remember. I hardly slept that night for the excitement of it. The first thing I did in the morning was to go to Breitkopf & Hartel's and buy the score. . . . I grew so enthusiastic over the symphony that I sent the score and parts to the Musical Fund Society of Boston, the only concert orchestra then in that city, and conducted by Mr. Webb. They could make nothing of the symphony, and it lay on the shelf for one or two years. Before my return from Europe in 1854, I think they finally played it. In speaking of it, Mr. Webb said to my father: "Yes, it is interesting; but in our next concert we play Haydn's "Surprise Symphony" and that will live long after this symphony of Schumann's is forgotten." Many years afterward I reminded Mr. Webb of this remark, whereupon he said "William, is it possible that I was so foolish?"

Only a few years before Mason's arrival in Europe, Schumann was so little appreciated that the clerks at Breitkopf & Hartel would laugh when he entered the store. One of them told him he considered him a crank and failure because his pieces remained unsold on the shelves and were in the way.

Mason received Schumann's musical autograph in 1850, a canon for male voices (shown at left):

Mason also called on Richard Wagner in 1852. At that time Wagner was known (not widely) as the composer of *Rienzi, The Flying Dutchman, Tannhäuser,* and *Lohengrin.* During their meeting Wagner talked enthusiastically about Beethoven, as recounted in Mason's memoirs:

> As he warmed up on the subject, he began to draw comparisons between Beethoven and Mendelssohn. "Mendelssohn," he said, "was a gentleman of refinement and high degree; a man of culture and polished manner; a courtier who was always at home in evening dress. As was the man, so is his music, full of elegance, grace, finish, and refinement, but carried without variance to such a degree that at times one longs for brawn and muscle. In Beethoven we get the man of brawn and muscle. He was too inspired to pay much attention to conventionalities. He went right to the pith of what he had to say, and said it in a robust, decisive, manly, yet tender way, brushing aside the methods and amenities of conventionalism, and striking at once at the substance of what he wished to express.

Mason did not leave Wagner's house without his musical autograph (shown at left):

Following studies with Alexander Dreyschock in Prague, Mason in 1853 decided to visit Liszt enroute to Leipzig. The butler who opened the door at the Altenburg mistook him for a wine merchant, but after presenting his card, Liszt exclaimed: "Nun, Mason, Sie lassen lange auf sich warten!" ("Well, Mason, you let people wait for you a long time!")

Liszt had been expecting him for four years now! Managing to pull himself together in light of this revelation, Mason was invited into the drawing room where Liszt said, "I have a new piano from Érard of Paris. Try it and see how you like it." Mason recounts the rest of the story in his memoirs:

> He asked me to pardon him if he moved about the room, for he had to get together some papers which it was necessary to take with him, as he was going to the palace of the grand duke. I felt intuitively that my opportunity had come. I sat down at the piano with the idea that I would not endeavor to show Liszt how to play, but would play as simply as if I were alone. I played "Amitié pour Amitié," a little piece of my own which had just been published by Hofmeister of Leipsic.
>
> "That's one of your own?" asked Liszt when I had finished. "Well, it's a charming little piece." Still nothing was said about my being accepted as a pupil. But when we left the Altenburg, he said casually, "You say you are going to Leipsic for a few days on business? While there you had better select your piano and have it sent here. Meanwhile I will tell Klindworth to look up rooms for you."
>
> I can still recall the thrill of joy which passed through me when Liszt spoke these words.

Liszt took no money from his pupils, nor did he give lessons in the strict sense. His idea was that the pupils he accepted should be far enough advanced to practice without routine instruction. Liszt loved to entertain and many were the distinguished artists, musicians, and poets who constantly visited him.

Mason was one of three pupils at the time, one of the others being Karl Klindworth with whom he formed a lasting friendship. Occasionally Hans von Bülow would make an appearance (having left Weimar not long before Mason's arrival). Every Sunday at eleven o'clock, the famous Weimar String Quartet would play in the grand rooms of the Altenburg, with Liszt occasionally joining in. Mason described Liszt's playing in his memoirs:

> Time and again at Weimar I heard Liszt play. There is absolutely no doubt in my mind that he was the greatest pianist of the nineteenth century. Liszt was what the Germans call an Erscheinung—an epoch-making genius. Rubinstein said to Mr. William Steinway in 1873: "Put all the rest of us together and we would not make one Liszt."

Mason continues:

> The difference between Liszt's playing and that of others was the difference between creative genius and interpretation. His genius flashed through every pianistic phrase, it illuminated a composition to its innermost recesses. . . .

In his memoirs Mason recalled the physical appearance of Liszt as he looked in 1854:

The best impression of Liszt's appearance at that time is conveyed by the picture which shows him approaching the Altenburg. His back is turned; nevertheless, there is a certain something which shows the man as he was better even than those portraits in which his features are clearly reproduced. The picture gives his gait, his figure, and his general appearance. There is his tall, lank form, his high hat set a little to one side, and his arm a trifle akimbo. He had piercing eyes. His hair was very dark, but not black. He wore it long, just as he did in his older days. It came almost down to his shoulders, and was cut square at the bottom.

Mason was present when the first meeting of Liszt and Brahms took place in 1853. Liszt had sent word up to "the boys" (as he called his students) that he expected a visit from a great new talent who was to be accompanied by the violinist, Eduard Remenyi.

Mason picks up the story:

The next morning, on going to the Altenburg with Klindworth, we found Brahms and Remenyi already in the reception room with Raff and Pruckner. . . . I strolled over to a table on which were lying some manuscripts of music. They were several of Brahms's yet unpublished compositions, and I began turning over the leaves of the uppermost in the pile. It was the piano solo "Op. 4, Scherzo, E Flat Minor," and, as I remember, the writing was so illegible that I thought to myself that if I had occasion to study it I should be obliged first to make a copy of it. Finally Liszt came down, and after some general observation he turned to Brahms and said: "We are most interested to hear some of your compositions whenever you feel inclined to play them."

Brahms, who was evidently very nervous, protested that it was quite impossible for him to play while in such a disconcerted state. . . . Liszt, seeing that no progress was being made, went over to the table, and taking up the first piece at hand, the illegible scherzo, and saying, "Well, I shall have to play," placed the manuscript on the piano desk.

We had often witnessed his wonderful feats in sight-reading, and regarded him as infallible in that particular, but, notwithstanding our confidence in his ability, both Raff and I had a lurking dread of the possibility that something might happen which would be disastrous to our unquestioning faith. . . . But he read it off in such a marvelous way—at the same time carrying on a running accompaniment of audible criticism of the music—that Brahms was amazed and delighted.

A little later someone asked Liszt to play his own sonata, a work which was quite recent at that time, and of which he was very fond. Without hesitation, he sat down and began playing. As he progressed he came to a very expressive part of the sonata, which he always imbued with extreme pathos, and in which he looked for the especial interest and sympathy of his listeners. Casting a glance at Brahms, he found that the latter was dozing in his chair. Liszt continued playing to the end of the sonata, then rose and left the room.

January

27

28

29

30

31

ERNST VON DOHNÁNYI (1877-1960)

THE HUNGARIAN DOHNÁNYI WAS A FRIEND of William Mason and was not part of the Appledore colony. Dohnányi, who was twenty-three years old in 1900, went on to achieve great success as a pianist, conductor, and composer. He was a schoolfellow of Béla Bartók's in Bratislava, and his music had a great influence on the young Bartók, who eventually outgrew this influence in becoming one of the twentieth century's greatest composers. Dohnányi was responsible as pianist or conductor for many of Bartók's world premieres, including the *Dance Suite* in 1923. He was professor of music and composition at Florida State University for many years.

EVERETT SHINN (1873-1958)

THIS ENTRY IS UNSIGNED, but the treatment of the eyes and the theatrical subject matter clearly identify the work as Shinn's. Shinn, the youngest of the early twentieth century group of American realist painters known as The Eight, was dazzled throughout his life by the glamour of the theater. He was at his artistic best when depicting show girls, clowns, or musicians. His paintings are included in the collections of the Whitney Museum of American Art and the Art Institute of Chicago.

Shinn may have visited Appledore. Unfortunately, the fire of 1914 that destroyed the Appledore Hotel also destroyed the guest books, so a clear record of all the guests who visited Appledore is unavailable.

February

1

2

3

4

5

6

7

February

8

9

10

11

12

13

14

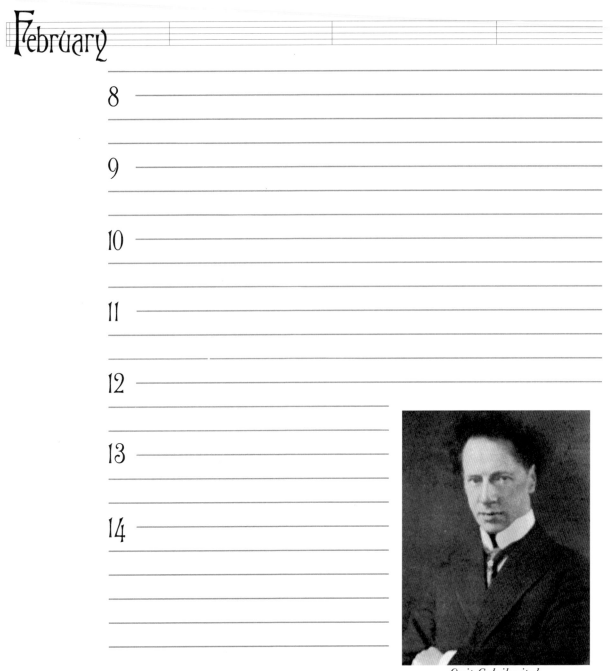

Ossip Gabrilowitsch

FRIDAY. FEB

1

Gavotte

To Mr. William Mason with best wishes for a merry Christmas

Ossip Gabrilowitsch.

OSSIP GABRILOWITSCH (1878-1936)

GABRILOWITSCH, THE RUSSIAN PIANIST, was one of Theodor Leschetitzky's most famous pupils. Gabrilowitsch probably never visited Appledore, but instead would have written this daybook entry while making his successful American debut in 1900. William Mason described his playing as "masterly, combining as it did genuine musical quality, intelligence in phrasing, and great brilliancy, as well as poetry in interpretation." Gabrilowitsch married Mark Twain's daughter and settled permanently in the States, where he conducted the Detroit Symphony from 1918 to 1936.

February

15

16

17

18

THE SUNRISE NEVER FAILED US YET
BY CELIA THAXTER

Upon the sadness of the sea
The sunset broods regretfully;
From the far lonely spaces, slow
Withdraws the wistful afterglow.

So out of life splendor dies;
So darken all the happy skies;
So gathers twilight, cold and stern;
But overhead the planets burn;

And up the east another day
Shall chase the bitter dark away;
What though our eyes with tears be wet?
The sunrise never failed us yet.

The blush of dawn may yet restore
Our light and hope and joy once more.
Sad soul, take comfort, nor forget
That sunrise never failed us yet!

Celia Thaxter with son John

WEDNESDAY FEB

6

The sunrise never failed us yet.

Cara C. Haynes,

CAROLINE COVENTRY HAYNES

THE NEW ENGLAND ARTIST, whose drawing of Portsmouth, New Hampshire can be found in the month of July, here quoting from Celia Thaxter's popular poem *The Sunrise Never Failed Us Yet*. The full poem is included at left.

PRIMARILY REMEMBERED for his outstanding conducting, Thomas was also a first-rate violinist who along with William Mason, Joseph Mosenthal, Carl Bergmann (subsequently replaced by Frederick Bergner), and George Matzka formed a string quartet in 1855 that offered chamber music concerts in Dodsworth's Hall in New York City. This group performed for the first time in America many new works including the *Grand Trio in B Major* by Brahms.

This daybook entry from Thomas refers to the third concert of the eighth season of the Mason and Thomas Quartet. It is reprinted exactly as written by Thomas, including the spellings used by the German-born musician.

(For more on Theodore Thomas see the daybook entry for September 4.)

The Mason and Thomas Quartet
Left to right: George Matzka, Joseph Mosenthal, Frederick Bergner, Theodore Thomas, William Mason

Tuesday, February 10th, 1862-1863
The 3rd soirée of Mason and Thomas had the following programme:

Quartett, C Major, No. 2	Cherubini
Trio, D Major, Op. 70, No. 1	Beethoven
Quartett, A Major, Op. 41, No. 3	Schumann

A programme as interesting and fresh today as 38 years ago. The weather was very cold, under zero, and in the Largo of the Trio the gass gave out—we continued playing for sometime, but finally had to stop. The "Geister" (the Beethoven Piano Trio referred to here was called by the Germans the "Geister Trio") did not assist us! Do you remember the fact! ha! ha! ha!

Es ist schon lange her. Theodore Thomas

February

19

20

21

22

23

24

25

MARGARET RUTHVEN LANG (1867-1972)

THE DAUGHTER OF B.J. LANG, the influential New England organist and choral director, Margaret Lang was one of the first American women to compose large works for orchestra. She wrote three concert overtures, two of which were performed by the Theodore Thomas and Boston Symphony orchestras. Her compositions were often played in Celia Thaxter's parlor. She lived to be 104 years old, and was honored with a special tribute by the Boston Symphony Orchestra three days before her 100th birthday.

February

26

27

28

29

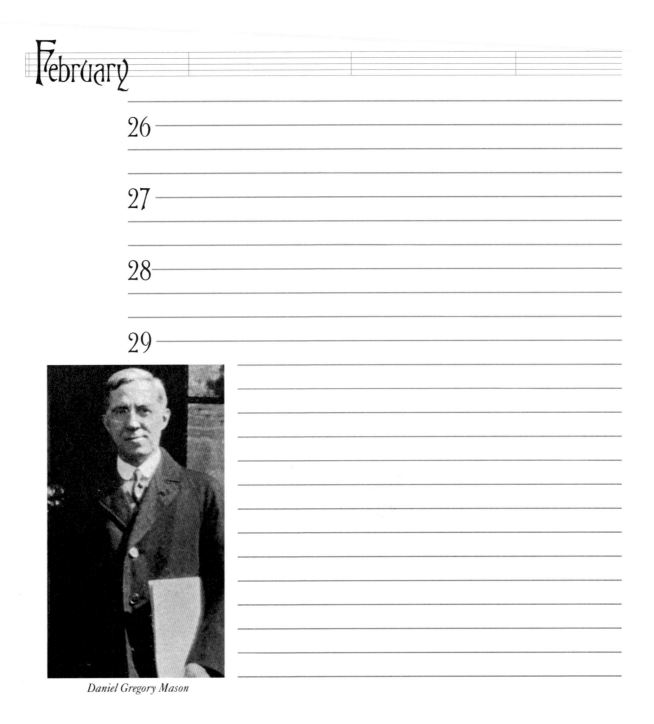

Daniel Gregory Mason

TUESDAY - FEB - **26**

Circumstances never favor the man who has not already surmounted them.

Daniel Gregory Mason.

DANIEL GREGORY MASON (1873-1953)

WILLIAM MASON'S NEPHEW, who became a prominent figure in American music during the first half of the twentieth century. Mason's First Symphony premiered in 1916 in Philadelphia with Leopold Stokowski conducting, and received subsequent performances by Ossip Gabrilowitsch in Detroit and Bruno Walter in New York. Mason was MacDowell Professor of Music at Columbia University from 1929 to 1940. In addition to his composing, he wrote several successful books about music.

FREDERICK CHILDE HASSAM (1859-1935)

THE ARABIC FLAVOR OF HIS SURNAME notwithstanding, Frederick Childe Hassam was born of Yankee descent on both branches of his family. His earliest ancestors in Salem, Massachusetts, had gone by the name Horsham, but the name became corrupted under Colonial misspelling. Hassam took pride in the fact that he could claim common ancestry on his paternal side with painter William Morris Hunt and architect Richard Morris Hunt, and on his maternal side with Nathaniel Hawthorne.

As a young boy growing up in the Boston suburb of Dorchester, Hassam displayed an aptitude for making small watercolors. In 1876, he took a job in the accounting department of the Boston publisher, Little, Brown, where his supervisor noted his facility at drawing and steered him toward a career in art. Hassam left Little, Brown to work as an apprentice to a wood engraver, George Johnston, where he quickly assumed responsibility for producing the original designs that were turned into wood engravings used by the printers. Among his earliest assignments was the design he provided for the masthead of the *Marblehead Messenger* in 1876.

With this experience under his belt, Hassam found opportunities for free-lance work in the burgeoning magazine-illustrating branch of American art. Winslow Homer had been providing the cover designs for *Harper's Weekly* with great success, and Hassam followed his lead in producing illustrations for *Harper's* and the *Century*. In 1892 Hassam's watercolors were featured in William Dean Howells's book *Venetian Life*, and two years later he provided the beautiful garden watercolors for Celia Thaxter's last book, *An Island Garden*.

Thaxter was an important influence on Hassam's career in a number of ways, not least of which was her ability to create the beautiful garden that served as the subject of many of his best paintings. She also was the person who convinced him to drop the name Frederick and use the more impressive sounding name Childe Hassam. In the Childe Hassam Papers at the Archives of American Art, a letter from Hassam written in 1933 gives the background to his newfound name:

Childe Hassam painting on Celia Thaxter's piazza

When I was not much past twenty I met Celia Thaxter who liked as so many others did (Miss Jane Hunt sister of William was another) to paint in watercolors. She said to me one day "You should not, with an unusual name like yours, fail to take advantage of its unique character—There is a young Englishman who has just written some remarkably good stories of India. He has married an American girl, a Miss Balestier of Brattleboro, Vermont. His name is Joseph Rudyard Kipling—but he has the literary sense to drop the prefix. If your name is to become known, as Jane Hunt and I think it will, it would be better without the F." That was quite early in my career and so I became Childe Hassam and I spent some of my pleasantest summers in the Isles of Shoals and in her salon there.

The work that Hassam produced during the twenty-six years he visited the Isles of Shoals is regarded by most art critics to be his finest. When Hassam was not painting Thaxter's garden, he could be found painting the rugged coastline in a style frequently compared to Monet's Brittany paintings. Hassam strongly resisted being pegged as an artist whose work was like any others', but the works of Monet most likely did influence him. When Hassam visited Paris between 1886 and 1889, he did not visit Monet at Giverny, but possibly this was simply because he did not want to spend the money to travel outside of Paris. He probably did see the initial exhibition of French impressionism in New York in 1886, which included Monet's work.

March

1

2

3

4

5

6

7

THURSDAY — MAR — 7

"Never trouble trouble
Till trouble troubles you."
              Lucy Derby Fuller.

LUCY DERBY FULLER

LUCY DERBY FULLER WAS A MEMBER of a prominent Salem, Massachusetts, family and a friend of Celia Thaxter. Thaxter's brother, Oscar Laighton, had fallen in love with her in 1880 only to be heartbroken when the relationship was cut short by Lucy, whose father had warned her to beware of entanglements on the Isles of Shoals. Lucy Fuller may have offered her lifelong friend Helen Keller the opportunity to submit her daybook entry, which appears on July 14.

March

8

9

10

11

12

13

14

Reflect, gentle reader, male or female
Every note of music is contained in this scale

ALBERT STERNER (1863-1946)

STERNER PROVIDED THREE ILLUSTRATIONS for the daybook. (See July 1 and November 1.) Born in London, Sterner painted portraits of many of America's best-known families. He believed in painting people as he saw them, and maintained that "most Americans really don't like themselves and want to look, or be made to look, like somebody else."

March

15

16

17

18

19

20

21

22

23 _____
_____

24 _____
_____

25 _____
_____

26 _____
_____

27 _____
_____

28 _____
_____

29 _____
_____

30 _____
_____

31 _____
_____

ROSS STERLING TURNER (1847-1915)

TURNER PRODUCED TWO WORKS for the daybook. (See September.) This entry is unsigned, but the way the letter "R" in "April" is written with the sloping descender, and the use of the same colors as seen in the signed September entry, identify the work as Turner's. He was a good friend of Celia Thaxter, William Mason, and Childe Hassam, and his landscape paintings were an early influence on Hassam. A fine example of his work is the watercolor *A Garden Is a Sea of Flowers*, which is in the Boston Museum of Fine Arts collection.

April

1

2

3

4

5

6

7

April

8

9

10

11

12

13

14

CONTRIBUTOR UNKNOWN. The original consists of a small photo of a spaniel pasted onto the page surrounded by decorative, ornate ribboning. A charming entry in keeping with the spirit of the Victorian Era.

April

15

16

Oscar Laighton

SUNDAY - APR. **7**

Appledore

Dearest, my heart is like the sea!
Surging with every gale that blows,
Longing for winds that bring the rose
The happy Summer Time and thee.

Oscar Laighton

OSCAR LAIGHTON (1839-1938)

CELIA THAXTER'S BROTHER, who along with her other brother, Cedric, operated the Appledore Hotel during its heyday in the 1880s and 1890s. Oscar dabbled as an artist (his schooner sketch appears at left) and he also wrote some verse. His book *Ninety Years at the Isles of Shoals* offers modern students a useful account of the Laighton family's years at the Isles of Shoals.

April

17

18

19

20

21

22

23

FREDERICK BERGNER

BERGNER TOOK CARL BERGMANN'S PLACE in the Mason and Thomas Quartet as cellist shortly after the group was assembled in 1855. The reason for Bergmann's departure from the group was due to the friction that had developed between Theodore Thomas and himself. Bergmann had been conductor of the New York Philharmonic Society and naturally assumed a position of leadership in the quartet. The young Thomas was also a gifted conductor, however, and in the end the two could not work together within the small confines of one quartet.

April

24

25

26

27

28

29

30

FRIDAY - APR - 26

Time brought me many another
        friend
That loved me longer
New love was kind, but in the end
Old love was stronger

Years come and go.. No new year yet
Hath slain December
And all that should have cried, forget!
Cries but — Remember

GUSTAVE SCHIRMER

GUSTAVE SCHIRMER (1864-1907)

GUSTAVE SCHIRMER WAS THE SON OF THE FOUNDER of the famous music publishing house, G. Schirmer, Inc. The poem he is quoting is *Not Yet* by Victorian poet Mary Elizabeth Coleridge. Mary Coleridge was a descendant of the great British poet, Samuel Taylor Coleridge. This is the complete poem.

MAY

PHOEBE PICKERING JENKS (1847-1907)

PHOEBE JENKS WAS BORN IN PORTSMOUTH, New Hampshire, and may have visited the nearby Isles of Shoals. She lived in Boston for several years where she worked as a successful portrait painter. Her best portraits were of women and young girls.

May

1

2

3

4

5

6

7

May

8

9

10

11

12

13

14

15

16

17

18

19

20

21

22

23

24

May

25

26

27

28

29

30

31

ALWIN SCHROEDER (1855-1920)

SCHROEDER SERVED AS FIRST CELLIST with the Boston Symphony Orchestra during its formative years, from 1886 until 1903. He was one of the many foreign musicians who made significant contributions to American music during the late 1800s. Following his years with the Boston Symphony, he joined the Kneisel Quartet, a very successful chamber music group active at the turn of the century.

SCHUMANN'S SONATA IN A MINOR
(Mit Leidenschaftlichem Ausdruck)
BY CELIA THAXTER

The quiet room, the flowers, the perfumed calm,
 The slender crystal vase, where all aflame
The scarlet poppies stand erect and tall,
 Color that burns as if no frost could tame,
The shaded lamplight glowing over all,
 The summer night a dream of warmth and balm.

Outbreaks at once the golden melody,
 "With passionate expression!" Ah, from whence
Comes the enchantment of this potent spell,
 This charm that takes us captive, soul and sense?
The sacred power of music, who shall tell,
 Who find the secret of its mastery?

Lo, in the keen vibration of the air
 Pierced by the sweetness of the violin,
Shaken by thrilling chords and searching notes
 That flood the ivory keys, the flowers begin
To tremble; 'tis as if some spirit floats
 And breathes upon their beauty unaware.

The stately poppies, proud in stillness, stand
 In silken splendor of superb attire:
Stricken with arrows of melodious sound,
 Their loosened petals fall like flakes of fire;
With waves of music overwhelmed and drowned,
 Solemnly drop their flames on either hand.

So the rich moment dies, and what is left?
 Only a memory sweet, to shut between
Some poem's silent leaves, to find again,
 Perhaps, when winter blasts are howling keen,
And summer's loveliness is spoiled and slain,
 And all the world of light and bloom bereft.

But winter cannot rob the music so!
 Nor time nor fate its subtle power destroy
To bring again the summer's dear caress,
 To wake the heart to youth's unreasoning joy,—
Sound, color, perfume, love, to warm and bless,
And airs of balm from Paradise that blow.

WEDNESDAY—
MAY—

29

"Whence comes the enchantment of this potent spell,
This charm that takes us captive, cool and sense!
The sacred power of music, who shall tell,
Who find the secret of its mastery?"

Ever Sincerely Yours — Maud Hassam

MAUD HASSAM

CHILDE HASSAM'S WIFE, MAUD, here quoting from Celia Thaxter's poem
Schumann's Sonata in A Minor. William Mason introduced many of Schumann's works to
American audiences, and Schumann was one of Thaxter's favorite composers. The full
poem appears at left.

JUNE

IGNAZ MARCEL GAUGENGIGL (1855-1932)

GAUGENGIGL SPECIALIZED IN FINELY DETAILED DRAWINGS such as the two that appear in this book. (See December.) Born in Bavaria, Gaugengigl was trained in Munich at the Royal Academy in 1874. Ludwig II commissioned him to paint *The Hanging Gardens of Semiramis*. Following studies in Paris and Italy, Gaugengigl settled in Boston in 1878 where he painted many of Boston's most prominent citizens. One of his best-known paintings is *Portrait of Man and Dog*, which is in the Boston Museum of Fine Arts collection.

June

1

2

3

4

5

6

7

June

8

9

10

11

12

13

14

SATURDAY-
JUNE-

1

Good morning, dear old friend! If you got bad weather, don't blame me for that... There is for you a bright and sunny, constant and warm affection in my heart.

I. J. Paderewski

IGNACE JAN PADEREWSKI (1860-1941)

"Good morning dear old friend! If you got
bad weather, don't blame me for that. . . . There
is for you a bright and sunny, constant and
warm affection in my heart."

PADEREWSKI WAS THE MOST WIDELY PUBLICIZED and idolized pianist of the post-Liszt era. He was the first great drawing card in America, and earned an estimated ten million dollars during his career, which reached its heights at the turn of the century.

Crowds would flock to hear him, with swooning female admirers lining up to catch a glimpse of their hero.

He was as much great showman as virtuoso. His physical appearance was an alluring combination of wild abandon and regal refinement. He projected a noble manner from behind the piano as he peered out into the audience with a distant, melancholy expressiveness that spoke volumes of unrequited love. Women would line up to behold the hands insured for a hundred thousand dollars. Hysterical throngs would rush to the pier to see him off for Europe, as recounted in the following excerpt from the *New York Sun* of April 23, 1896:

Ignace Jan Paderewski

As the White Star steamship Teutonic moved majestically out from the pier yesterday noon, there was heard above the blaring of the band, the shouting of the seamen, the general tumult incidental to the occasion, a high chorus of shrill tones. It was the farewell of Paderewski's feminine admirers. . . . Previous to the parting chorus, they had mobbed the long-suffering pianist, pressing against him, shaking his hands, giving him flowers, pestering him for autographs, and begging him in tearful voices to come back again soon.

Paderewski always took the utmost care in maintaining his noble image. His touring entourage included a private railroad car, his personal chef and butler, a private physician, his wife and *her* aides, and a host of other comforts more befitting a king than a touring musician.

Beneath the showman's exterior lived a genuine musical genius, the rare breed of virtuoso that comes around only once every half-century. Paderewski came to America in 1891, making his debut in the newly opened Carnegie Hall on November 17, 1891, with Walter Damrosch conducting the orchestra. The early reviews from the musical establishment were not overwhelmingly favorable, and William Mason played a key role in swinging popular opinion in Paderewski's favor at a time when his fame still hung in the balance. Mason's enthusiastic letter to the *Evening Post*, which was later expanded into a *Century* article, provided the official musical stamp of approval that the hordes of lovestruck female fans needed to justify so many nights out at the concert hall admiring their hero's "sensitive touch." Mason wrote:

> It seems to me that in the matter of touch, Paderewski is as near perfection as any pianist I have ever heard, while in other respects he stands more nearly on a plane with Liszt than any other virtuoso since Tausig. . . . [His playing] possesses that subtle quality expressed in some measure by the German word *Sehnsucht*, and in English as "intensity of aspiration." This quality Chopin had, and Liszt frequently spoke of it. It is the indefinably poetic haze with which Paderewski invests and surrounds all that he plays which renders him so unique and impressive among modern pianists.

The crowds he drew during the 1890s were the largest yet witnessed in the brief history of American concert giving. Audiences would not allow him to leave the stage, often calling for encores that lasted over an hour. Crowds waited at railroad crossings to see his private car pass. One female fan received three autographs from Paderewski, "one to frame and hang in my bedroom, one to paste inside the piano to improve its tone, and one to carry with me always."

During the early years of the twentieth century, Paderewski's fame began to dwindle, with many music critics complaining of his uneven and unsatisfactory performances. Possibly the wear and tear of the concert circuit was taking its toll, or more likely the critics were in need of a new celebrity to feast upon. Whatever the reasons, Paderewski returned to his native Poland in 1909 where he became director of the Warsaw Conservatoire. In 1919, he became one of the first premiers of Poland, for whose freedom he had actively campaigned.

He made a brief return in 1923 as a performer, but he was clearly past his prime. He was elected president of Poland's newly formed provisional government in 1940, and died the following year in Switzerland.

Few virtuosi have enjoyed a comparable level of popularity as Paderewski. His style and dignity, along with his outstanding pianistic talent, made him one of the greatest performing artists of all time.

June

15

16

17

18

19

20

21

22

EDWARD ALEXANDER MacDOWELL (1861-1908)

EDWARD MacDOWELL WAS THE MOST POPULAR AMERICAN COMPOSER active during the late nineteenth century. He wrote several large works for orchestra, but is best remembered for his smaller piano pieces. MacDowell was quoted in the January 1915 issue of the *Musical Quarterly* as having said: "It's one thing to write works for the orchestra, and another to get them performed. There isn't much satisfaction in hearing a thing played once in two or three years. If I write large works for the piano I can play them myself as often as I like."

In 1896, when Columbia University established its music department, MacDowell was named as its first professor of music. Subsequently, the Edward MacDowell Chair of Music was created in honor of its first incumbent.

Many of MacDowell's works for piano, including *Sea Pieces*, *Woodland Sketches*, and *Sonata Tragica* (a favorite of the Appledore guests), are currently available on recordings.

June

23

24

25

26

27

28

29

30

HOWARD BROCKWAY (1870-1951)

BROCKWAY WAS PART OF THE GROUP of America's first orchestral composers that included Edward MacDowell, John Knowles Paine, George Chadwick, and Horatio Parker. At a time when American composers struggled to be taken seriously, Brockway saw his compositions performed abroad to considerable acclaim. Wilhelm Gericke (see entry for September 20), conductor of the Boston Symphony Orchestra from 1884 to 1889, performed Brockway's *Sylvan Suite* for orchestra as well as several of his other works.

ALBERT STERNER (1863-1946)

STERNER CAME TO THE UNITED STATES when he was nineteen and was first employed as a scenery painter at the Grand Opera House in Chicago. He left Chicago for New York where he provided illustrations for *Harper's* and *Scribner's*, but resented "the limitations set on art by editors who try to force fresh talent into the accustomed mold."

July

1

2

3

4

5

6

7

July

8

9

10

11

12

13

14

SAMUEL PROWSE WARREN (1841-1915)

> So (my) fugue broadens and thickens,
> Greatens and deepens and lengthens,
> Till (you) exclaim—"But where's music, the dickens?"

WARREN WAS A CANADIAN ORGANIST who in 1865 came to New York where he served as organist-choirmaster in All Soul's Church and later in Grace Church. He was one of the founding members of the American Guild of Organists.

ONE OF THE MOST INSPIRING PERSONALITIES of the twentieth century here quoting from an unidentified source using the raised writing board she used at the time this entry was written. In 1900, the year the original daybook was compiled, Keller was just beginning her first year at Radcliffe College.

Keller had been afflicted with a rare disease when she was nineteen months old that left her blind and deaf. It was through the efforts of Alexander Graham Bell, the inventor of the telephone, that young Helen Keller came to the attention of the Perkins School for the Blind in Watertown, Massachusetts. Bell, whose wife was deaf, had suggested to Keller's father that he contact Michael Anagnos, the director of the Perkins School for the Blind, since he was aware of the remarkable work the school had done on behalf of their prize pupil, Laura Bridgman. Following this advice, Helen was enrolled at the school where Perkins alumna Annie Sullivan assumed responsibility for her education. Helen and Annie formed a lifelong bond that endured the many hardships they faced together as they made their way in the world.

From the day she first arrived at Perkins, Keller displayed a passion to learn that quickly set her apart from the other pupils. Her insatiable curiosity and implicit trust in all around her were characteristics that endeared her to many of the leading men and women of her time. Helen's love of poetry led her to write to Oliver Wendell Holmes and John Greenleaf Whittier, who were charmed by her irresistible sweetness and became early champions of her rise to prominence.

She quickly became a cause célèbre within the Boston Brahmin philanthropic community. The turn of the century saw Boston at the pinnacle of its golden years as America's cultural center, and Keller described Boston as "The City of Kind Hearts, a city of friends and lovers of liberty." Helen's unspoiled qualities of goodness and benevolence helped to teach other, more fortunate, people valuable lessons about seeking the higher goals of gratitude and contentment.

Her early fame in Boston soon spilled over into New York literary circles, where she caught the attention of Mark Twain and William Dean Howells. Keller had met these writers at the home of Laurence Hutton, whose daybook entry appears for September 17. Hutton and his wife established a trust fund for Helen and her teacher, Annie, which helped pay for much of Helen's education. Hutton, who was a distinguished writer and bibliophile, offered the following description of Helen shortly after meeting her for the first time:

> I cannot give expression to, nor can I altogether explain to myself, the impression she made upon us. We felt as if we were looking into a perfectly clear fresh soul,

SUNDAY - JULY -

14

"The present time is
like a nearer sail;
Fretted and torn and
soiled with stormy tears —
Anchored far out beyond recalling, hail
All sails look white across the sea years"

Helen Keller

without reserve. Here was a creature who absolutely knew no guile and no sorrow, from whom all that was impure and unpleasant had been kept. . . . She was a revelation and an inspiration to us. And she made us think and shudder, and think again. She had come straight from the hands of God. . . . She seems to have a sixth sense. She receives and understands somehow what of course she cannot hear. She laughed at everything. She smiled at every one. Everything was pleasant to her. Everybody was good.

Upon meeting Mark Twain, Keller wrote: "Mr. Clemens told us many entertaining stories, and made us laugh till we cried. I think he is very handsome indeed. . . . Teacher said he looked something like Paredeuski. (If that is the way to spell the name.)" Twain later said of Helen: "The two greatest characters of the 19th century are Napoleon and Helen Keller. Napoleon tried to conquer the world by force and failed. Helen tried to conquer the world by power of mind—and succeeded."

When Keller was twenty-one years old and a sophomore at Radcliffe, she signed a contract with *Ladies Home Journal* to write the story of her life in five installments. These installments were published in book form by Doubleday Page in 1903 and launched Helen's career as a writer. Richard Watson Gilder called the book "unique in the world's literature . . . the most remarkable of modern times." Publication of the book in Great Britain by Hodder & Stoughton caught the interest of Queen Victoria. Mark Twain wrote: "I am charmed with your book— enchanted. You are a wonderful creature, the most wonderful in the world." The book became an international classic and established Helen as a persuasive voice for the many causes she would champion during her life.

At the time of her graduation from Radcliffe, Keller summed up what her college experience had meant to her:

Helen Adams Keller

> College has breathed new life into my mind and given me new views of things, a perception of new truths and of new aspects of the old ones. I grow stronger in the conviction that there is nothing good or right which we cannot accomplish if we have the will to strive. The assured reality and nearness of the end of my school days fills me with bright

anticipation. The doors of the bright world are flung open before me and a light shines upon me, the light kindled by the thought that there is something for me to do beyond the threshold.

Helen would step through "the doors of the bright world" in making it even brighter, as she would toil with unfailing energy in helping to bring world attention to the needs of the deaf and blind, women, and blacks. She was instrumental in securing equal rights for the blind in the Social Security Act of 1935. And she persuaded President Roosevelt to appropriate the funds needed for installing 5,000 talking book machines in the Library of Congress. Her speeches around the world raised money for many social organizations, not least of which was the American Foundation for the Blind.

It is in large part due to her pioneering work that our modern society is as aware as it is of the needs of the physically challenged in providing equal access and opportunity to all that our culture has to offer.

July

15

16

17

18

19

20

21

22

23

24

25

26

27

28

July

29

30

31

CAROLINE COVENTRY HAYNES

A SKETCH OF PORTSMOUTH, NEW HAMPSHIRE, by the New England artist who may have visited the Isles of Shoals. Haynes studied in Paris with Alfred Stevens and Courtois, and exhibited at the New York Watercolor Club, the Boston Art Club, and the Philadelphia Art Club. She was one of the first presidents of the National Association of Women Painters and Sculptors.

LAURA COOMBS HILLS (1859-1952)

HILLS SPENT MUCH OF HER LIFE IN NEWBURYPORT, Massachusetts, and may have visited Appledore, where her fellow Newburyporter, John Appleton Brown, spent many summers. Hills studied in New York with William Merritt Chase, and became a popular miniaturist and pastelist specializing in portraits and floral still-lifes. The Boston Museum of Fine Arts owns her *Larkspur, Peonies, and Canterbury Bells*, painted in 1915.

August

1

2

3

4

5

6

7

August

8

9

10

11

12

13

14

FRIDAY – AUG. – 2

Reflect, gentle reader, male or female
Every note of music is contained in this scale

Harold Bauer

HAROLD BAUER (1873-1951)

THE LONDON-BORN BAUER WAS THE RARE EXCEPTION to the rule that every great pianist must start as a child prodigy. He began as a violinist, switching to the piano when he was twenty. By the year 1900 he was well-established as a successful concert pianist. Bauer once wrote that nobody could ever know exactly how a composer intended a piece to be played solely by reading the music "for the simple reason that musical notation permits of only relative, and not of absolute, directions for performance, and must therefore be an approximation which no two people can interpret precisely in the same way."

August

15

16

17

18

19

20

21

GASTON MARIE DETHIER (1875-1958)

DETHIER WAS NOT ASSOCIATED WITH APPLEDORE, but was active in New York as an organist and teacher. He graduated from the Liège Conservatory at age seventeen with gold medals in piano and organ, and first prize in fugue. Along with his brother, Eduoard, he gave many organ recitals in New York.

August

22

23

24

25

26

27

28

WEDNESDAY-
AUG- **21**

*It is the lot of friends to part:
We meet as travellers of a day,
An interchange of heart with heart,
And then — each turns and goes his
way.*

Dudley Buck

DUDLEY BUCK (1839-1909)

DUDLEY BUCK WAS THE FIRST AMERICAN TO COMPOSE large choral works. By the mid-nineteenth century religious music in America had evolved from the simple psalms of the Puritans to the more musical hymns of Lowell Mason and Thomas Hastings. Buck carried the evolutionary process forward with his prolific output of choral works. His cantata *Scenes from the Golden Legend*, which was set to Longfellow's poem, won the $1,000 prize at the 1880 Cincinnati Music Festival. Buck's book, *Illustration in Choir Accompaniment, with Hints on Registration*, published in 1877, has served as a valuable guide for several generations of choir leaders and organists.

29

30

31

FAITH
(My Lighthouse)
BY CELIA THAXTER

Fain would I hold my lamp of life aloft
  Like yonder tower built high above the reef;
Steadfast, though tempests rave or winds blow soft,
  Clear, though the sky dissolve in tears of grief.

For darkness passes, storms shall not abide;
  A little patience and the fog is past.
After the sorrow of the ebbing tide
  The singing flood returns in joy at last.

The night is long and pain weighs heavily,
  But God will hold the world above despair.
Look to the East, where up the lucid sky
  The morning climbs! The day shall yet be fair!

FRIDAY - AUG - 30

From Celia Thaxter.

Fain would I hold my lamp of life aloft
Like yonder tower built high above the reef;
Steadfast, though tempests rave or winds blow soft,
Clear, though the sky dissolve in tears of grief.

For darkness passes, storms shall not abide;
A little patience and the fog is past.
After the sorrow of the ebbing tide
The singing flood returns in joy at last.

G. M. Schirmer.

G. M. SCHIRMER

THIS IS NOT WRITTEN BY GUSTAVE SCHIRMER whose entry appears for April 26th, but is from another member of the family. The passage quoted is from Celia Thaxter's poem *Faith*. The full poem appears at left.

MEXICO! R·T· SEPTEMBER.

ROSS STERLING TURNER (1847-1915)

TURNER MAINTAINED A STUDIO ON APPLEDORE, having first met Celia Thaxter during the 1880s when she had been one of his art students in Boston. At Appledore, Turner painted Thaxter's garden in a similar style to Hassam's. Turner traveled often looking for new subject matter, and his love of the sea took him to Venice, the Caribbean, and Mexico, the subject of this entry for September.

September

1

2

3

4

5

6

7

"Never Trouble trouble
Till trouble troubles you."
  Lucy Derby Fuller

IT WAS THROUGH THE PIONEERING EFFORTS OF THEODORE THOMAS that almost all of America's major cities had symphony orchestras in place by 1900. The chronology of the major American symphonies is as follows:

> 1842: Philharmonic Society in New York
> 1865: Harvard Musical Association in Boston
> 1878: New York Symphony
> 1880: St. Louis Orchestra
> 1881: Boston Symphony Orchestra
> 1891: Chicago Symphony Orchestra
> 1900: Philadelphia Orchestra

Thomas was the first outstanding conductor active in the United States. His Theodore Thomas Orchestra, started in 1864, was the first American orchestra made up of permanent, full-time musicians. The Thomas Orchestra maintained a rigorous schedule in performing in all of America's major cities, and it was due to its success that Boston, Philadelphia, Chicago, and other cities realized there was sufficient demand to warrant the establishment of their own permanent orchestras.

Thomas displayed early in his career a stubborn determination—often against the will of his audiences and critics—to include major works by Beethoven or Mozart on a program made up of other less challenging pieces. By means of his clever ability in combining popular music with less accessible new works, Thomas was able to raise the level of musical appreciation in America despite the objections of his audiences. In his memoirs, William Mason discussed the early genius Thomas showed for building a program: ". . . he rapidly developed a talent for making programs by putting pieces into the right order of sequence, thus avoiding incongruities. He brought this art to perfection in the arrangement of his symphony concert programs."

The enormous impact of Thomas's pioneering work can be measured in part by the fact that in 1870 he finally felt he could include an entire symphony on a program without losing the interest of his

Theodore Thomas

WEDNESDAY-
SEP-

4

A good day for
a Clambake

Theodore Thomas.

audience. Imagine attending a performance today of Beethoven's Fifth Symphony and only hearing the first movement! This was the sorry state of classical music in America at the time Thomas was acting as missionary on behalf of many of the great European composers of the nineteenth century.

Among the many works he introduced to American audiences were: Berlioz's *Harold in Italy*, Brahms's Second and Third Symphonies, Bruckner's Fourth Symphony, the Sibelius Second Symphony, and several works of Beethoven, Tchaikovsky, and Mozart.

In 1891, Thomas was offered the conductorship of the first season of the newly formed Chicago Orchestra. He quickly made many enemies within the Chicago press, who resented his obstinacy in program policy and his generally unyielding nature. An excerpt from the *Chicago Herald* of May 11, 1893, is here offered as a fine example of abusive journalism: "He is a small despot by nature, a dull and self-opinionated man. . . . A constitutional want of generosity, an unscrupulous resistance to reasonable appeals from every quarter, and a thrift that has looked out for himself no matter who suffered in consequence . . . a pragmatic curmudgeon . . . totally without prestige. . . ." Apparently, the Chicago press longed to hear *Yankee Doodle* instead of Mozart. Despite the personal onslaught, Thomas declined an offer to leave Chicago for the more receptive environment of Boston as conductor of the Boston Symphony Orchestra, and remained in Chicago until his death in 1905.

His final great act for Chicago was in leading the fundraising drive for the building of the new Orchestra Hall in 1904. He conducted only five concerts in the new building before his death and was succeeded by Frederick Stock, who built the orchestra into one of the country's finest symphonies.

Thanks largely to one man, Theodore Thomas, by the beginning of the twentieth century musical life in America had improved vastly over its impoverished state during the Civil War years.

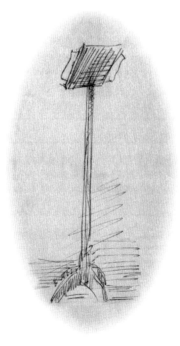

September

8

9

10

11

12

13

September

14

15

16

17

18

19

BENJAMIN JAMES LANG (1837-1909)

LANG WAS A PROMINENT FIGURE IN NEW ENGLAND MUSIC during the latter half of the nineteenth century. He was primarily known for his work as organist and choral director. He served as organist and conductor of the Handel and Haydn Society in Boston. Among his more notable pupils were Arthur Foote, Ethelbert Nevin, and his own daughter, Margaret, whose daybook entry appears for February 15.

September

20

21

22

23

24

25

TUESDAY - SEP - **17**

Your music hath charm ... cooks... ... ...

Laurence Hutton.

LAURENCE HUTTON (1843-1904)

LAURENCE HUTTON WAS AN INFLUENTIAL WRITER, educator, and editor of the time who visited Appledore often. An astute judge of character, he had the following to say about Celia Thaxter:

> So long as she lived she went but little into the world, and almost the only world she knew was the small fraction of the world which came to her. . . . Celia reigned not only in the little society of intelligent people she drew around her, but also in the hearts of the fisherfolk who inhabited the little group of islands known as the Shoals. Among them she was queen indeed. . . . They were a colony of simple, hard-working Swedes (Norwegians), to whom she was physician, patron, pastor, friend. She nursed them when they were ill; named their babies; shared their joys and sorrows.

September

26

27

28

29

30

Andante tranquillo.

FRIDAY· SEP·

20

Musica serva dei'

Wilhelm Gericke

WILHELM GERICKE (1845-1925)

In 1881, Henry L. Higginson, a Boston banker, founded the Boston Symphony Orchestra, the first outstanding permanent orchestra in America. The German-born Gericke became conductor in 1884 and molded the young orchestra into the finest orchestra then active in America. A demanding drillmaster who expected perfection from all his players, Gericke served as conductor of the Boston Symphony Orchestra until 1889.

FREDERICK CHILDE HASSAM (1859-1935)

THE ARTISTIC OUTPUT OF CHILDE HASSAM and Celia Thaxter reflected their common concerns, even though they worked in different mediums. Hassam's Appledore paintings capture many of nature's fleeting moments—moving clouds, shimmering rocks, and fading light—subject matter that also fascinated Celia Thaxter as evidenced in her writings, including her first published poem, *Land-Locked*, which appears at right:

LAND-LOCKED
BY CELIA THAXTER

Black lie the hills; swiftly doth daylight flee;
  And, catching gleams of sunset's dying smile,
  Through the dusk land for many a changing mile
The river runneth softly to the sea.

O happy river, could I follow thee!
  O yearning heart, that never can be still!
  O wistful eyes, that watch the steadfast hill,
Longing for level line of solemn sea!

Have patience; here are flowers and songs of birds,
  Beauty and fragrance, wealth of sound and sight,
  All summer's glory thine from morn till night,
And life too full of joy for uttered words.

Neither am I ungrateful; but I dream
  Deliciously how twilight falls to-night
  Over the glimmering water, how the light
Dies blissfully away, until I seem

To feel the wind, sea-scented, on my cheek,
  To catch the sound of dusky flapping sail
  And dip of oars, and voices on the gale
Afar off, calling low,—my name they speak!

O Earth! the summer song of joy may soar
  Ringing to heaven in triumph. I but crave
  The sad, caressing murmur of the wave
That breaks in tender music on the shore.

Thaxter wrote this poem when she was twenty-five and living with her husband in their Newtonville, Massachusetts home. Following their marriage, they divided their time between the mainland and the islands, a circumstance that Celia probably had not foreseen when she consented to marrying Levi Thaxter, and a contributing factor to their eventual separation.

From the time Childe Hassam first visited Appledore during the mid-1880s until Thaxter's death in 1894, Thaxter assisted him in seeing all the beauty to be found on her special island. A more qualified guide can hardly be imagined, as Celia introduced

Hassam to the many views he would come back to paint year after year until 1916.

The warm friendship they shared came to an abrupt end in 1894 when Celia suddenly passed away. This was the second tragic loss Hassam had experienced at Appledore, the first being the apparent suicide in 1879 of his kinsman, painter William Morris Hunt, who was found face down in the Appledore Pond by Celia.

Hassam helped to carry Celia's coffin to her grave, an account of the funeral offered below as described by William Mason:

> During the summer of 1894 Mrs. Thaxter seemed as well and active as usual, still working in her garden, still the lively center of her group of friends and admirers. One day she did not appear, nor the next, and then we heard she had peacefully passed away.

> None who were at Appledore then will easily forget that 26th day of August, nor the day she was buried on her island home.

> The funeral service was held in the well-known sitting-room; the address was made by her old friend the Rev. Dr. James De Normandie, and, by request of her sons, I played Schumann's "Romance in F Sharp" and Dvorak's "Holy Mount." . . .

> When the simple service was over the coffin was followed by her old and faithful friends and the island fishermen to the grave by that of her father and mother. The long procession of people, through the gray mist, winding in and out along the rocky way, the leaden sky and sea, the hushed voices of the children, usually ringing out so merrily from rocks and hotel piazzas, accentuated the sense of our loss.

> At the grave, all lined with bayberry and flowers, the coffin was lowered, and each of those present came forward and laid upon it a few of the flowers she loved so dearly.

Hassam stayed away from Appledore following Thaxter's death, instead traveling to Paris, Naples, and Rome. When he returned to New York in 1897, he decided to become independent of the Society of American Artists, and at a meeting in New York on December 17, 1897, Hassam, along with J. Alden Weir and John H. Twachtman, founded a new organization known simply as The Ten. The other members were Willard L. Metcalf, Robert Reid, Thomas W. Dewing, Edward E. Simmons, Frank W. Benson, Edmund C. Tarbell, and Joseph R. De Camp.

The primary purpose for leaving the Society of American Artists had to do with Hassam's disdain for the hodgepodge of exhibitions they were putting together, typically lumping many different styles together in one confusing show. Hassam was an ardent supporter of James McNeill Whistler's aesthetic theory, which called for achieving artfully controlled color effects. While Celia Thaxter had been alive, he had only to look around her parlor at the carefully coordinated flower arrangements to see theory in practice.

October

1

2

3

4

5

6

7

8

Circumstances never favor the man who has not already surmounted them.

Daniel Gregory Mason.

October

9

10

11

12

13

14

15

16

17

18

19

20

21

22

23

24

October

25

26

27

28

29

30

31

HORATIO WILLIAM PARKER (1863-1919)

Music is written in notes and uttered in tones. Other things (such as for instance lectures and literature) are frequently if not usually said from the purpose of true music.

HORATIO PARKER'S CHORAL COMPOSITIONS, most notably *Hora Novissima* (1893), earned him international recognition during his lifetime. His choral writing was especially popular in England, where in 1902 he received an honorary degree of music from Cambridge University. In 1894 he became chairman of the Music Department at Yale University, where he remained until his death in 1919. His most notable pupil at Yale was Charles Ives (1874-1954), who went on to become the first American composer whose international fame endured well beyond his lifetime. (Ives also studied organ at Yale with Dudley Buck.)

ALBERT STERNER (1863-1946)

STERNER KNEW BOTH EVERETT SHINN AND CHILDE HASSAM and possibly one of these artists offered him the opportunity to provide his illustrations for the original daybook. Sterner studied at Julien's Academy and École des Beaux Arts in Paris. His works are in the collections of the Metropolitan Museum of Art, the Carnegie Institute, the Fogg Museum at Harvard University, and the Victoria and Albert Museum in London.

November

1

2

3

4

5

6

7

The sunrise never failed us yet.

Cara C. Haynes.

November

8

9

10

11

12

13

14

15

FRANK VAN DER STUCKEN (1858-1929)

FRANK VAN DER STUCKEN WAS THE FIRST ORCHESTRAL CONDUCTOR to present programs exclusively made up of American composers' works. He did this in the 1880s in New York and again in 1889 at the Paris Exposition. He was a prolific composer; Liszt performed his prologue to Heine's tragedy *William Ratcliff* at Weimar, an excerpt from which appears as this entry. In 1895 van der Stucken became conductor of the newly formed Cincinnati Symphony Orchestra, where he frequently included works by America's emerging generation of composers alongside the masters of the Old World.

November

16 —

17 —

18 —

19 —

THE ORIGINAL DAYBOOK PAGE consists of an actual photo of Celia Thaxter's cottage pasted down on the page. Thaxter's cottage was the site of many summers of entertaining conversation and camaraderie. The photo shown opposite is of the interior of Celia's parlor.

JOHN PAINE FIRST VISITED APPLEDORE in the mid-1860s and was a regular visitor until the time of his death in 1906. Paine and William Mason could often be found entertaining the guests at the grand piano in Celia Thaxter's parlor. Paine had arranged to have the piano delivered to Celia's parlor shortly after his first visit to the island, and one can only marvel at the difficulties involved in moving a grand piano from the mainland to Appledore at a time before the advent of the automobile.

Paine is recognized as "the dean of American composers," as he was the earliest of America's musicians to compose large orchestral works. A native of Portland, Maine (which also takes pride in claiming Henry Wadsworth Longfellow as a native son), Paine studied organ with Hermann Kotzschmar, the German musician who settled in Portland after coming to America in 1848 with the Saxonia Band. Following studies with Kotzschmar, Paine spent three years in Berlin studying organ with August Haupt, one of the greatest organists then living. With the advantages of such superior early training, Paine returned to America in 1861 where he became the country's foremost organist.

In 1860, the Music Hall in Boston imported a magnificent F. Walcker & Sons organ from Germany, and thousands went to hear Paine's recitals at which he introduced compositions of Bach to American audiences. In 1861 he was organist in the West Church in Boston, but resigned the following year to become organist and chapel master at Harvard University. At Harvard, Paine delivered many lectures on music free of charge until 1875, when the first chair of music to be established in an American university was created for him. In much the same way that Lowell Mason forced music into the American public school curriculum, Paine did the same on the university level. During the forty-three years he served at Harvard, he educated many talented American composers, including Arthur Foote, Daniel Gregory Mason, and John Alden Carpenter.

In 1867 his first large work, *A Mass in D*, was performed in Berlin, an event marking the first foreign performance of an American composer's work. In 1873, Paine's *Oratorio of St. Peter* premiered in his native Portland, Maine. John Fiske, an eminent essayist and critic of the time, wrote of this performance: "This event is important not only as the

John Knowles Paine

FRIDAY - NOV - 22

Lieber Herr Mauer,

It is with my best wishes and warm regards that I subscribe myself

Ever yours

John K. Paine

first appearance of an American oratorio, but also as the first direct proof we have had of the existence of creative musical genius in this country. . . . With the exception of Mr. Paine, we know of no American hitherto who has shown the genius or the culture requisite for writing music in the grand style."

Paine's First Symphony was played by the Theodore Thomas Orchestra in Boston in 1876. The Boston Symphony Orchestra, under Wilhelm Gericke's direction, performed many of Paine's compositions during the 1880s, including his *Island Fantasy*, which was Paine's attempt to translate the power and mystery of the sea as suggested to him by two of John Appleton Brown's paintings of the Isles of Shoals which were on display in Celia

November

20

21

22

Thaxter's parlor. Paine's composition, *Oedipus Tyrannus*, written in 1881, won the gold medal at the unveiling ceremony of the Wagner monument in Berlin in 1904.

Paine's achievements as America's first symphonic composer and pioneering music professor place him at the forefront of American musical history. At the time of his death in 1906, the music critic of the *Outlook* wrote: "His most distinguished quality was his thorough knowledge of his subject. . . . His pupils remember the severe standards for musical composition, his extreme indulgence for the student, his whimsical eccentricities, his naivete, his likable egotism, his absorption in his art and his fine simple spirit and character." Arthur Foote wrote: "John Knowles Paine, the first American-born musician to compose music that placed him in the first rank. We younger men all looked up to him. He has never had the true recognition that was his due."

As was true of the works of the majority of his contemporaries, Paine's works were performed with declining frequency following his death. The way had been paved for America's subsequent generation of composers—twentieth-century giants Charles Ives, Aaron Copland, and George Gershwin most notably—composers who built upon the successes of their musical "parents" in taking American music to new heights. Unlike most of his contemporaries, the passage of time may prove beneficial in evaluating the musical merits of Paine's compositions, as evidenced in part by the many recent recordings of his works. His first two symphonies are available for modern audiences in performances by Zubin Mehta and the New York Philharmonic, and *Oedipus Tyrannus* and *Oratio of St. Peter* are also currently available.

ARTHUR WILLIAM FOOTE (1853-1937)

FOOTE WAS A PUPIL OF JOHN KNOWLES PAINE at Harvard and was part of the group of New England composers active in the 1890s who were collectively known as the "Boston Classicists." His output was considerable for an American composer of the time, with eight works for orchestra and thirty works for organ to his credit. Theodore Thomas played his *Serenade in E* at the World's Fair in 1893, and Foote credited Thomas with introducing many of his works to American audiences. Foote was one of the founders of the American Guild of Organists, serving at one time as its president.

November

23

24

25

26

27

28

29

30

EDGAR STILLMAN KELLEY (1857-1944)

ALONG WITH HORATIO PARKER, John Knowles Paine, George Chadwick, and Edward MacDowell, Kelley was one of America's most talented composers active in the late 1800s, and one who helped gain international respectability for American music. At a time when most American musicians resisted being dismissed as "American composers" and therefore, by inference, lesser composers, Kelley offered his view of what American music should be: "The American composer should apply the unusual principles of his art to the local and special elements of the subject-matter as they appeal to him, and then, consciously or unconsciously, manifest his individuality, which will involve the expression of mental traits and moral tendencies peculiar to his European ancestry, as we find them modified by the new American environment."

DEC.

IGNAZ MARCEL GAUGENGIGL (1855-1932)

THIS FINELY DETAILED DRAWING perfectly enhances the musical flavor of the daybook. Gaugengigl was a visitor to Appledore, probably coming to the island through his association with Childe Hassam. Gaugengigl was one of Hassam's earliest teachers in Boston. His works are in the collections of the Metropolitan Museum of Art and the Boston Museum of Fine Arts.

December

1

2

3

4

5

6

7

December

8

9

10

11

12

13

14

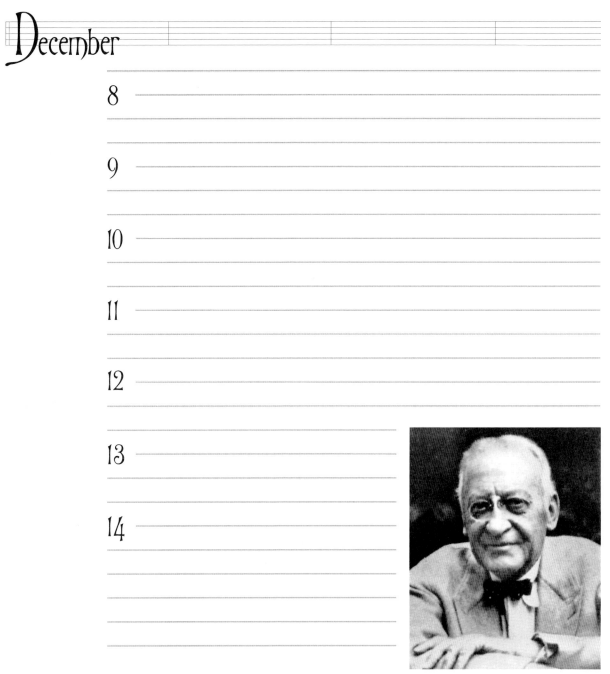

Arthur Batelle Whiting

SATURDAY – DEC. 7

Arthur Whiting

Heard melodies are sweet, but those un-
heard
Are sweeter: therefore, ye soft pipes,
play on;
Not to the sensual ear, but, more en-
deared,
Pipe to the spirit ditties of no tune.
— Keats

Arthur Batelle Whiting (1861-1936)

WHITING WAS ONE OF THE MORE TALENTED COMPOSERS of the Boston Classicists group. His works were performed by all the major orchestras in America at the turn of the century, with several of his compositions also having foreign performances at a time when few Americans were heard overseas. He and his wife visited Appledore on many occasions.

December

15

16

17

18

TERESA CARREÑO (1853-1917)

CARREÑO WAS ONE OF THE MOST CHARISMATIC PERFORMERS of the second half of the nineteenth century. Born in Venezuela, she stormed the musical world as a child of nine, where her tempestuous personal manner was only surpassed by the wild abandon of her piano playing. She was invited to play for President Lincoln at the White House, where she promptly complained about the piano. She became friends with William Mason, and he recalled late in life his earliest memories of her: "I well remember the impression she made upon me at that time (early 1860s)— both from her artistic playing and her charming appearance in 'pantalets,' the fashion for children of that day."

WEDNESDAY-
DEC. 18

Andante — etc

Teresa Carreño

May each day of many years to
come bring you all joy and happiness!

Carreño studied with Anton Rubinstein. She had the physical strength and technical ability to play many of the large piano works of the time. Hans von Bülow described her as "the most interesting pianist of the present age."

In 1892, she married the talented musician Eugene d'Albert, her third marriage and one that lasted only three years. An amusing review in a German newspaper at the time she was married to d'Albert reported: "Frau Carreño yesterday played for the first time the second concerto of her third husband at the fourth Philharmonic concert." One of her pupils was Edward MacDowell, and in 1888 she performed the world premiere of his D minor piano concerto.

The view from Celia Thaxter's piazza

WEDNESDAY –
DEC –
25

"Appledore"

Here, where the waves encircle the
wave washed Shore like a caressing
hand and the murmur of the water
reaches me with almost the Sweetness
of your dear voice, I will tell you
how much I love you

Oscar Laighton

THE UNSPOILED BEAUTY OF THE ISLES OF SHOALS has held a strange fascination
for visitors from the time of their first recorded sightings in the 1600s. In 1614 John Smith
named the Isles of Shoals "Smyths Iles" and described them as follows in his *Description
of New England*: "The remarkablest Iles and mountains for Landmarks are these. . . .
Smyths Isles are a heape together, none neere them." He went on to describe New
England: "And of all foure parts of the world that I have yet seen not inhabited, could I
have but the meanes to transport a Colonie, I would rather live here than any where."

Christopher Levett, writing in 1628 in *A Voyage to New-England*, wrote: "The first place
I set my foote upon in New England was the Iles of Shoulds, being Ilands in the Sea,

about two Leagues from the Mayne. Upon these Ilands I neither could see one good timber tree, nor so much good ground as to make a garden."

Celia Thaxter, who 250 years later would make a splendid garden, wrote in her first work of prose, *Among the Isles of Shoals*:

> Swept by every wind that blows, and beaten by the bitter brine for unknown ages, well may the Isles of Shoals be barren, bleak, and bare. At first sight nothing can be more rough and inhospitable than they appear. The incessant influences of wind and sun, rain, snow, frost, and spray, have so bleeched the tops of the rocks, that they look hoary as if with age . . . so forbidding are their shores, it seems scarcely worth while to land upon them—mere heaps of tumbling granite in the wide and lonely sea.

Thaxter also described in *Among the Isles of Shoals* her first voyage to the island as a girl of four:

> It was at sunset in autumn that we were set ashore on that loneliest, lovely rock, where the lighthouse looked down on us like some tall, black-capped giant, and filled me with awe and wonder. At its base a few goats were grouped on the rock, standing out dark against the red sky as I looked up at them. The stars were beginning to twinkle; the wind blew cold, charged with the sea's sweetness; the sound of many waters, half bewildered me. Some one began to light the lamps in the tower. Rich red and golden, they swung around in mid-air; everything was strange and fascinating and new. We entered the quaint little old stone cottage that was for six years our home.

With Thaxter's death in 1894 came an extended run of bad luck that eventually brought down the final curtain on the Appledore era. Increased competition from the many new summer resorts along the Atlantic seaboard began to cut into the hotel's profits. Oscar Laighton struggled to keep the hotel solvent, but in 1900 the bank foreclosed on the property. An attempt to parcel off pieces of the island failed, and in 1914 a disastrous fire burned the hotel and many of the cottages to the ground, turning to ash in one quick day what had been a lively center for American arts for half a century.

For much of the twentieth century the Isles of Shoals served as a U.S. Navy target range for canon fire. In recent years the Isles of Shoals have been an ideal outpost for the marine biology program jointly run by Cornell University and the University of New Hampshire. In 1978, Professor John Kingsbury of Cornell restored Celia Thaxter's garden using the original plans from *An Island Garden*, and it is now possible for visitors to see the replicated garden in front of the remains of Celia's cottage.

December

19

20

21

22

23

24

25

December

26

27

28

29

30

31

TUESDAY — DEC — 31

Thy friends greet thee,
Thy friends love thee,
Thy friends wish thee joy in the
        coming year.
And bid thee — Auf Wiedersehen
                    Julia Laighton

JULIA STOWELL LAIGHTON, THE COMPILER OF THE ORIGINAL DAYBOOK, here bidding "Auf Wiedersehen" for the year. Julia Laighton was married to Celia Thaxter's brother, Cedric, who passed away in 1899, the year before the compilation of the original daybook. Cedric was the inspiration for Frances H. Burnett's character Little Lord Fauntleroy.

BIBLIOGRAPHY

Curry, David Park. *Childe Hassam: An Island Garden Revisited*. New York and Denver, 1990.

Edwards, George Thornton. *Music and Musicians of Maine*. Portland, Maine, 1928.

Elson, Louis C. *The History of American Music*. New York, 1904.

Fairbrother, Trevor, et al. *The Bostonians: Painters of An Elegant Age, 1870-1930*. Boston Museum of Fine Arts catalog, Boston, 1986.

Faxon, Susan, et al. *A Stern and Lovely Scene: A Visual History of the Isles of Shoals*. University of New Hampshire exhibition catalog, Durham, New Hampshire, 1978.

Fields, Annie, and Rose Lamb, eds. *Letters of Celia Thaxter*. Boston and New York, 1895.

Hawthorne, Nathaniel. *The American Notebooks of Nathaniel Hawthorne*, edited by Randall Stewart. New Haven, Connecticut, 1932.

Hoopes, Donelson. *Childe Hassam*. New York, 1979.

Howard, John Tasker. *Our American Music*. New York, 1929.

Hutton, Laurence. *Talks in a Library with Laurence Hutton*. New York, 1905.

Laighton, Oscar. *Ninety Years at the Isles of Shoals*. Boston, 1930.

Lash, Joseph P. *Helen and Teacher*. New York, 1980.

Mason, Daniel Gregory. *Music in My Time and Other Reminiscences*. New York, 1938.

Mason, William. *Memories of a Musical Life*. New York, 1901.

Robinson, Frank T. *Living New England Artists*. Boston, 1888.

Rutledge, Lyman V. *The Isles of Shoals in Lore and Legend*. Boston, 1971.

Schonberg, Harold C. *The Great Conductors*. New York, 1967.

Schonberg, Harold C. *The Great Pianists from Mozart to the Present*. New York, 1963.

Schonberg, Harold C. *The Lives of the Great Composers*. New York, 1970.

Thaxter, Celia. *Among the Isles of Shoals*. Boston, 1873.

Thaxter, Celia. *Driftweed*. Boston, 1878.

Thaxter, Celia, et al. *The Heavenly Guest, with Other Unpublished Writings*, edited by Oscar Laighton. Andover, Massachusetts, 1935.

Thaxter, Rosamond. *Sandpiper: The Life and Letters of Celia Thaxter*. Francestown, New Hampshire, 1963.

Vallier, Jane E. *Poet On Demand: The Life, Letters and Works of Celia Thaxter*. Camden, Maine, 1982.

Young, Mahonri Sharp. *The Eight: The Realist Revolt in American Painting*. New York, 1973.

NOTE: All of the artwork used to decorate pages throughout (with the exception of the supplementary photographs identified on the copyright page) are taken from the original 1901 daybook, and are in most cases details from the above entries. If they are not cited above, it is because the contributor is unknown.

A NOTE ON PRODUCTION

*The text for this book is Caslon 540,
a typeface designed by William Caslon in the 1720s,
and considered the last of the Old Style typefaces.
Month names and dates are Glorietta,
introduced as Columbian in 1891
by American designer Herman Ihlenburg,
one of the most prolific of all Victorian type designers.*

*Composition and all prepress production
on Macintosh computers by ImageSet Design, Portland, Maine.*

*Printed and bound by
Horowitz/Rae Book Manufacturers, Inc., Fairfield, New Jersey.*

DESIGNED BY MARY REED